★ Pass the Buck ★

A Fun Song About the Famous Faces and Places on American Money

By Michael Dahl

Illustrated by Brandon Reibeling

Special thanks to our advisers for their expertise:

Tom Mega, Ph.D., Department of History
University of St. Thomas (Minnesota)

Susan Kesselring, M.A., Literacy Educator
Rosemount-Apple Valley–Eagan (Minnesota) School District

PICTURE WINDOW BOOKS
MINNEAPOLIS, MINNESOTA

Managing Editor: Bob Temple
Creative Director: Terri Foley
Editor: Kristin Thoennes Keller
Editorial Adviser: Andrea Cascardi
Copy Editor: Laurie Kahn
Musical arrangement: Elizabeth Temple
Designer: Melissa Voda
Page production: The Design Lab
The illustrations in this book were created digitally.

Picture Window Books

5115 Excelsior Boulevard
Suite 232
Minneapolis, MN 55416
1-877-845-8392
www.picturewindowbooks.com

Printed in the United States of America.

Library of Congress Cataloging-in-Publication Data

Dahl, Michael.
Pass the buck : a fun song about the famous faces and places on American money / Michael Dahl ; illustrator, Brandon Reibeling.
p. cm. – (Fun songs)
Summary: Relates the reasons why certain historical places and people have been honored by being depicted on American coins and paper money, interspersed with verses of original song lyrics to be sung to the tune of "This Old Man." Includes bibliographical references (p.) and index.
ISBN 1-4048-0132-4 (lib. bdg.)

1. United States—History—Miscellanea—Juvenile literature. 2. United States—History—Songs and music—Juvenile literature. 3. United States—Biography—Juvenile literature. 4. Paper money—United States—Juvenile literature. 5. Paper money—United States—Songs and music—Juvenile literature. 6. Coins, American—United States—Juvenile literature. 7. Coins, American—United States—Songs and music—Juvenile literature. [1. United States—History—Miscellanea. 2. United States—Biography. 3. Paper money. 4. Coins, American. 5. United States—History—Songs and music. 6. Paper money—Songs and music. 7. Coins, American—Songs and music.] I. Reibeling, Brandon, ill. II. Title.
E178.3 .D18 2003
973'.02—dc21

SING ONE! SING ALL!

It's the new historical ditty:

"Pass the Buck."

Sing along to the tune of "This Old Man."
Tell the tale of all the faces and places

on the money of today!

Many years ago, people in America were called colonists. The King of Great Britain ruled them. They got tired of his laws and ways. One British law said that colonists could not make their own money. Instead, they had to use British money. But there wasn't enough of it to go around. People had to use tobacco, beaver skins, and grain for money.

The colonists decided to fight for their freedom. They fought the British in a war that lasted from 1775 through 1783. During that time, they made their own money. The new money did not have pictures of British kings and queens on it. The money helped the colonists feel free from Britain. It did not work very well, though. People were afraid to use it.

They trusted money more after the war ended. New money always showed well-known people and places. This fun song tells the story of some American coins and paper money.

This old man, he's on one.
He was the first elected one.

George Washington was
the first American president.
Before that, he was
a leader in the
Revolutionary War.

He fought freezing cold and the Brits at Valley Forge.

Valley Forge was a winter camp where Washington stayed with his troops.

Guess his name! That's right! It's George.

7

Who's this crew? They're on two.
Each wears wig and buckled shoe.

They risked life and home and family. Every one signed the Declaration.

Men from all over met to talk about forming a new country. They signed the Declaration of Independence on July 4, 1776. It says that all people should be free.

Who's this guy on the nickel?
He saved his country from a pickle.

Where's this building on the hundred?
It's in Philly, if you wondered.

Folks there cried out,
"Let's have liberty for all!
Call it Independence Hall."

Independence Hall is the meeting place where the Declaration of Independence was signed. The hall stands in Philadelphia.

See that man on the other side?
Many ideas he supplied.

He invented swim fins, lightning rods, and then flew a kite. His name is Ben.

Ben Franklin was a statesman, an inventor, and a printer. He once flew a kite during a thunderstorm. He did this to prove that lightning was caused by electricity.

Who's that woman on the coin dollar?
Snow and mountains could not stall her.

Sacagawea was a Shoshone Indian. She and her husband helped explorers Lewis and Clark. Her baby is pictured with her on the coin.

She led Clark and Lewis.
Courage won her fame.
Sacagawea's her name.

Where's that state?
What's that date?
Each state makes our country great!

Each new quarter shows a scene
from one of the 50 states.
Each one has an extra date
printed on it.
The date tells when
that state became
part of the nation.

And our country's motto
is stamped on every one:
"Out of many,
we are one!"

E PLURIBUS UNUM money. The Latin words are printed on all "Out of many," comes one." Early leaders wanted people to know that the 13 colonies could make one great country.

CAESAR RODNEY

E PLURIBUS UNUM

1999

DELAWARE 1737

THE FIRST STATE

Pass the Buck

This old man, he's on one. He was the first e – lec – ted one. He fought

free –zing cold and the Brits at Val – ley Forge. Guess his name! That's right! It's George.

2. Who's this crew?
They're on two.
Each wears wig and buckled shoe.
They risked life and home and family. Every one
Signed the Declaration.

3. Who's this guy
On the nickel?
He saved his country from a pickle.
Who can shape the kind of government we need?
Jefferson! He will succeed!

4. Where's this building
On the hundred?
It's in Philly, if you wondered.
Folks there cried out, Let's have liberty for all!
Call it Independence Hall.

5. See that man
On the other side?
Many ideas he supplied.
He invented swim fins, lightning rods, and then
Flew a kite. His name is Ben.

6. Who's that woman
On the coin dollar?
Snow and mountains could not stall her.
She led Clark and Lewis. Courage won her fame.
Sacagawea's her name.

7. Where's that state?
What's that date?
Each state makes our country great!
And our country's motto is stamped on every one:
Out of many, we are one!

Did You Know?

Did you know that the Great Seal is printed on the back of the one-dollar bill? The seal shows a bald eagle. The eagle carries 13 arrows. It also carries an olive branch with 13 leaves and 13 berries. The numbers stand for the original 13 colonies. The bald eagle is the national bird of the United States.

Did you know that the place where money is made is called a mint? The U.S. Mint in Philadelphia was the first public building built for the new government of America. Horses powered the machines that made the first coins. Today there are mints in Philadelphia; Denver; San Francisco; Fort Knox, Kentucky; and West Point, New York.

Did you know that the first coin to show an African American was the half dollar? In 1946, the Booker T. Washington Memorial Half Dollar was made. Booker was born a slave. He is best known for helping black people live better lives after slavery ended. The back side of the coin shows his birthplace.

GLOSSARY

colonist—a person who lives in a new land but is ruled by people in a former land

freedom—the right to do and say what you like

government—the people who rule a country or organization

mint—where money is made

money—the coins and bills that people use to buy things

To Learn More

AT THE LIBRARY

Godfrey, Neale S. Neale S. Godfrey's Ultimate Kids' Money Book. New York: Simon & Schuster Books for Young Readers, 1998.

Spies, Karen Bornemann. Our Money. Brookfield Conn.: Millbrook Press, 2001.

Young, Robert. Money. Minneapolis: Carolrhoda Books, 1998.

ON THE WEB

The United States Mint: H.I.P. Pocket Change

http://www.usmint.gov/kids

Uses games and fun facts to explain coins

The Bureau of Engraving and Printing: Money Central Station

http://www.bep.treas.gov/kids/start.html

Uses games and fun facts to explain paper money

Fact Hound

Fact Hound offers a safe, fun way to find Web sites related to this book. All of the sites on Fact Hound have been researched by our staff.
http://www.facthound.com

1. Visit the Fact Hound home page.
2. Enter a search word related to this book or type in this special code: 1404801324.
3. Click on the FETCH IT button.

Your trusty Fact Hound will fetch the best sites for you!